AF610789

Carolle L. Bright

PEACE

The Twenty Miracles from God

Copyright © 2017 Carolle L. Bright.
Photo Copyright © 2017 Arne Glassbourg (photojournalist@bell.net)

All rights reserved. No part of this book may be reproduced, stored, or transmitted by any means—whether auditory, graphic, mechanical, or electronic—without written permission of the author, except in the case of brief excerpts used in critical articles and reviews. Unauthorized reproduction of any part of this work is illegal and is punishable by law.

ISBN: 978-1-4834-6782-5 (sc)
ISBN: 978-1-4834-6783-2 (e)

Library of Congress Control Number: 2017905018

Because of the dynamic nature of the Internet, any web addresses or links contained in this book may have changed since publication and may no longer be valid. The views expressed in this work are solely those of the author and do not necessarily reflect the views of the publisher, and the publisher hereby disclaims any responsibility for them.

Any people depicted in stock imagery provided by Thinkstock are models, and such images are being used for illustrative purposes only.
Certain stock imagery © Thinkstock.

Lulu Publishing Services rev. date: 05/26/2017

This book is dedicated to my son
and all that he loves.

Acknowledgements

In 2008 I self-published the book *A RIGHTFUL HEART* with www.lulu.com. I purchased 145 copies and sold half of them to my friends and acquaintances, and gave the rest away to people who needed inspiration in their lives.

In 2016, I decided it was time to market the book, so I bought my favorite publishing package with lulu and retitled the book *PEACE: The Twenty Miracles from God.* I could not have accomplished this project without lulu's incredible team of publishing professionals, and I knew I was in the best hands the entire time.

I am thankful for my family in always applauding my accomplishments, and personal friends who have supported me in welcoming *PEACE: The Twenty Miracles from God* to the world.

With gratitude,
Carolle L. Bright
February 20, 2017

Visit author: www.CarolleLBright.com

Table of Contents

As the bow of a ship
lines up and straightens its journey,
the human heart strengthens its direction.
Stay in tune with that which fulfills you,
for your needs make sounds
you cannot ignore.
Listen to their echoes
and direct yourself,
for your journey is waiting to be met.

Holy Spirit

Introduction

YOU ARE GOD'S MIRACLE

THIS BOOK IS for the broken-hearted and downcast and contains many miracles. They appear silently without thunderclaps and roaring winds to bring change. There are big miracles and little miracles, big changes and small changes. Within this world of tragedy, miracles are happening all the time. There is no warning that a miracle is coming, for it simply appears in peace and assurance. At times, miracles can be very disconcerting, and they can throw you for a loop.

"Miracles belong to each and every one of you,"
said God.
"Always keep these words close at hand.
The road to fulfillment is straight and bumpy,
but as long as you listen to My words
I will carry and guide you along the way.
You are never without Me."

Miracles are your dreams come true.
You are God's miracle come true.

God's messages were given to me to expand the consciousness of humanity and reveal its true nature of having a heart for God. This is a story about

God, my Creator and friend who loved me so much that no matter what I did, He never stopped loving me. There was a time in my life when I felt God's presence leave me. God never did. I turned away from God because I could not adjust to the tragic changes in my life.

After my son was born, and I felt God's presence, once again, I never fully returned to church, because I cherished the intimate relationship with Jesus alone, in silence. Talking with your best friend is only possible without distractions, and although I attended different churches occasionally, I never found one that encouraged an intimate relationship with God. Rather, God was to be revered as a paternal and forceful image that existed somewhere off into the distance. I knew God was much more than that, and I learned through prayer that the concept of having God in my life was through communicating with His Son, Jesus Christ.

I never fully understood the difference between God and Jesus Christ, except that one was the Father and the other was the Son. To me, God and Jesus were separate, yet the same thing. If Jesus was the Son of God, then He must be God too. Neither was I clear as to the exact function of the Holy Spirit, God's Comforter.

The majesty of God seemed incomprehensible to me. I felt that it seemed more effective if I spoke to Jesus directly, rather than to God. I often referred to Jesus as God in my prayers. It seemed my prayers were not answered specifically, and other things, which I did not ask for, came into my life to work out my situation. Frustrated and confused, the struggle in raising a child alone very often did me in. On becoming a single parent, the notion of getting what I desired was quickly eliminated and was exchanged for getting the basic needs met every month. The idea of everyday pleasures and good times, holidays and travel, never existed for me. I had to stop wanting and keep my life simple. The suffering opened up my heart, and God began speaking to me prophetically, loud and clear.

1

CHILDHOOD

I GREW UP in Vancouver, where I lived one block from a small lake, surrounded by trees, bushes, and peat bogs, and filled with catfish, bass, frogs, and ducks. Often after school, I would take my dog Penny to the lake, where we would spend the few hours left until suppertime. I learned to swim in the lake in the summertime, ice skate on it in the winter, and on the weekends, my friends and I would spend the entire day at the lake. If we felt brave, we would journey around it climbing the trees, weaving our way through the deep bushes, stepping around the peat bogs, or else jumping on them until we broke through.

In the summer holidays, we would swim in the lake all day long, and one of our favorite tricks was to jump into the warm bottomless peat bogs up to our armpits, climb out, and then run into the lake to wash off. From these outings, we would return home stinking, but never thought anything of it. We were proud of our algae colored green hair as we walked up the street, feeling that we had somehow conquered the lake. Getting dirty was part of our connection to it, and we had survived by not fearing it.

Every few years, a boy would accidentally drown, and it was always someone I did not know. They would dive off the raft and attempt to swim under it to the other side. Mostly, they would survive the trick, but occasionally one boy would die. I was relieved that I never witnessed a drowned boy pulled from the water. It caused me great sadness that my lake, which gave me so much fun and pleasure, could actually kill a swimmer. To me, the whole idea put darkness over the lake and depressed me for weeks. I concluded that the boy could not hold his breath long enough, and so I practiced holding my breath until I could swim underwater for a very long time. Eventually I was able to swim underwater from the shore to the raft, which was really quite far, and no one else was able to do this great fear. My friends were not interested in the whole idea, because they never worried about drowning. They were having too much fun fooling around and jumping off the raft as cannonballs.

Secretly, it was my intention to make sure that if I ever got stuck underwater, I could survive until rescued. After hearing the news of a drowning, I refrained from swimming to the raft. Instead, I swam closer to shore, until the dreaded feeling of death left me.

Often, we could feel the catfish brush by our bodies; it would sting a little, and we would voice the experience because we had survived it. I believed the catfish lived away from shore past the raft, on the north side of the lake, where we never ventured because past the raft was where they lived, along with other imagined creatures. These were bottom feeders, which could be made angry if we swam too close to the bottom and disturbed them. We never did, and we never saw them.

Besides having dangers, the lake became my refuge; the water always refreshed me and filled me with great solace. On a Saturday morning, if it was raining cats and dogs, (the rain was never cold) Penny and I would walk around the entire lake and return home completely soaked right through to the skin. The whole point of walking in the rain was to become dripping wet because it always felt good on my face and long hair, and I felt some sort of cleansing from it. Penny never minded it either; being part Labrador and part Collie, she always loved the water. We made a great team, and she was my companion to the lake, and I never went without her.

The lake also intrigued me because of its mysterious tranquility and beauty, and I had love and respect for it. As a small child, I believed in fairies and often would create fairy gardens from small plants and pieces of moss gathered from around the lake. I would gently put these fragments into a small box, and Penny and I would return home to the warm basement. In a larger box, I would create a special fairy garden, with a tiny bridge to a cozy place for the fairies to sleep in. I knew there were fairies because the plants always grew, and only fairies could do this magic. The fairies became my connection to nature, and the mysteries of the lake became my connection to God.

My grandparents lived a half hour's walk from our house. Often my older brother and I would spend the weekends there. My mother would pull me in a red wagon with Penny, and together we would trot to grandma's house. We always passed by the lake. I do not think that there was ever a time when I was away from the lake for more than a couple of days at a time, except when I grew older, and we went on our summer, two-week camping vacation through the interior of British Columbia.

I always felt lost during these holidays. We always traveled deep into the bush and barely saw any other people during that time. My dad loved to go into "The Bush" as deep and far away from civilization as possible, to explore and learn new things about nature. Every year we would go somewhere just as strange and isolated as the previous year. I was always so happy to return to my familiar home and to the lake, but these vacations taught me how much my father loved nature, and that was something we shared together.

2

CHILD OF GOD

WHEN I WAS seven, I was being outfitted at my grandparents' house, with a princess flower girl dress because my cousin was getting married. My stay-over bedroom was in the attic, and I had to climb up many narrow, steep stairs without any handrail. That was not too difficult, but the trip downstairs in the morning was terrifying for me. I gripped the wall as best I could, for fear if I slipped, I would be thrown to the bottom and killed instantly, dashed to smithereens.

On this particular occasion, my dress was being altered in the kitchen. When my mother and grandma were finished, they told me to go upstairs and change into my play clothes. Upon reaching the top of the stairs, I was drawn to a window facing the back of the house. Looking up to the sky, I felt a warm presence coming from that direction. I do not know for how long I stood there frozen in time.

The warm sense of love coming from that direction impressed upon me that I belonged somewhere else other than where I was standing in the attic. Coming out of this frozen state, I was floored with this revelation. I marched back downstairs holding up the bottom of my dress and without gripping onto the wall because I was more angry than afraid of falling. Promptly I walked up to my mother and asked her if I was adopted. She took it upon herself to find this idea very cute at first, until I repeated the question. Then she told me to stop being silly. This made me feel quite indignant because she did not appreciate my sense of betrayal. I marched back upstairs without holding onto the wall and became lonely and very depressed.

Later I concluded that my mother was right since everyone said I looked just like her, so she had to be my real mom. However, from that day at the window, I always felt deep down inside that I belonged somewhere else and to someone else.

When I turned eight, my mother decided that she wanted to be baptized. Often the new minister would come to the house. We would eat yummy cookies, and everyone would chat and laugh. I never understood what they were laughing about, but I really enjoyed the cookies that were not the usual peanut butter kind, but a very fancy and sweet delicious sort.

The prerequisite for baptism was to go to church, so we began going to church. Eventually the minister stopped coming to our house. The delicious cookies changed into the peanut butter kind, and my mother was baptized.

I remember it so clearly, she in her gold satin dress with black velvet trim; it was the first time I ever saw my mother kneel and look so humble with her bowed head. I never forgot the image. I felt that God had touched her. After the baptism, my parents seldom went to church except for me because I loved Sunday school and was hungry for it. So every Sunday morning I would walk to church by myself, singing songs about Jesus.

In Sunday school, we spent a lot of time coloring pictures and learning about Jesus and the books of the Bible. He intrigued me because He portrayed deep abiding love for all and had the amazing ability to forgive His enemies. This was of particular interest to me, for I could never figure out how He was able to do this. If I could, then I would be able to handle my brother, who always teased and played nasty tricks on me. He was older, bigger, and smarter than I was, and he always won. We always fought because it seemed that he constantly bugged me. This really caused my mother concern and many headaches. Often she would send me to the store for aspirin, the really strong kind.

I had friends from school who were also in my Sunday school class. One particular friend played the piano at a church one block away, because her father was the minister. My mother told me that my friend's church was a little different from ours, but she never explained what the difference was, and I never asked. I thought about it for a few weeks and finally decided that I would visit my friend's church and find out what this mystery was all about. I was young but felt brave, and this was the first time I attended a new church. I felt strange sitting with the adults but had confidence that I would understand the sermon and discover the great mystery of their church.

Well, I never did understand the sermon, as everything went right over my head, and I felt disappointed about that. I was so bored that I felt like falling asleep. I had become so completely rooted in the pew, and my back ached from sitting straight for what seemed like hours. I thought it best that I should leave before I fell forward.

I was beginning to think everything was too complicated for me; as I stood up to leave, the minister raised his voice and said, "If you do bad things, your tongue will turn black, and you will go to hell." Since I was the only one standing, it appeared he was directing this message to me. I knew I was not perfect but could not for the life of me think of any terrible things I had ever done. I flew out of that church, ran home wailing and crying to my mother that my tongue was going to turn black, and I was sure to go to hell.

I knew that hell was a place where you got eaten up by hideous creatures, and it was beyond me why anyone would ever want to go there! So I never thought about it. However, that experience was very traumatic for me. I learned for the first time that there was something evil God knew about and had something to do with. I decided that I was never going to find out what it was. The idea of God as warm and loving changed into something to fear, and He became a deeper mystery to me.

3

QUAKER HERITAGE

MY GRANDPA WAS also a mystery to me. He grew the most spectacular flower garden with roses and chrysanthemums, some being over six feet tall. He smoked cigars, played the piano and sang, and there was always a waft of sweet-smelling cigar smoke throughout the house. When he played the piano, I watched him from peeking around the corner since I was shy and afraid of him. He rarely spoke to me; when the dreaded time came for me to kiss his whiskered cheek before going up to the attic to bed, he would softly say good night and then look me squarely in the eyes. I knew he knew something that I did not want to know about. His sense of greatness was too overwhelming for me. I feared that one day his great secret would be revealed to me and change me forever.

My grandma was small and funny; I loved her very much. She made the most amazing homemade candy. At Easter time, she made Turkish Delight, a "melting in your mouth" type of candy for the adults and children, and bacon and eggs and peas out of icing sugar. They were colored and looked like the real thing, and it took us two days to eat them because they were so sweet. We had a sugar high for the entire weekend.

Around Easter, her cactus would bloom a flower for one day only and for us to see this was a miracle from God. We were always at her house to see the cactus flower bloom. If it was to bloom the next day, I was always so excited and could not wait to see God's miracle the next morning. Sure enough, the cactus flower bloomed the entire day and then died the next. I could never understand why God would make us wait a whole year to see a cactus flower bloom for one day, and this added more to the secrets of God.

My mother and grandma also made the Christmas rum fruitcake every year, and it was so delicious. I remember one particular Christmas in my grandma's kitchen when they were laughing and couldn't stop. Strangely, they even offered me a drink of rum, and as a child I could not understand why they would do this. Apparently while preparing the cake, which involved cutting nuts and dried fruit and other stuff that seemed to take the entire day, they had been sampling the rum. By the late afternoon, they were drunk. From that day, at each Christmas we were reminded of that particular time when my mother and her mother got drunk in the pantry.

There were many mysteries in my family. I tried to understand them, but as a child, I was not able to grasp a lot of things going on around me. They seemed to laugh at situations I did not find amusing. Particularly, there was one occasion when my parents and grandparents would all introduce themselves to other people, and everyone would laugh. For years, I never understood this, but later on I figured it all out and this is how it went. My father and mother were married. During this time, my father's father was divorced, and my mother's mother was divorced also. Eventually, they married each other and became my grandparents.

There was a sense of greatness about my grandpa, something big like God, and I always felt uncomfortable around him. I knew he was very smart in math because I was told that, and he could write shorthand. He never spoke to me very often, and, being shy, I never got to know him. At least once a year, my grandma would proudly remind me that Grandpa often had tea with Queen Victoria. I did not know why he would have done that, and this added to the greater mystery of my grandpa.

When my grandma was three, she danced for Queen Victoria and was presented with a doll. I knew that my grandpa was around the same age as she was, and I could not imagine that he danced for Queen Victoria. I thought it strange that a young boy would have tea with Queen Victoria unless he had a secret gift and possibly performed magic tricks, which, I concluded, must be true since I knew he was brilliant. I never questioned my grandma about it because I did not want to hurt her feelings since she appeared to think I understood the whole story.

I never did understand because no one ever told me, and I did not want to question her, in case I found out something that would affect me forever, and so I let it go. I always felt that if any mystery was opened up, my life would be changed forever. Later, I discovered that it was not my grandpa but his great-great-grandfather, John Bright, a Quaker and member of Parliament, who had tea with Queen Victoria.

My grandpa's nobleness came from John Bright, one of the world's greatest orators, who brought reform to England and believed in the sanctity of human life. As a member of the Peace Party and advocate of free trade and nonintervention abroad, he was firmly rooted in the idea that international arbitration was possible rather than going to war and dying for king and country. "Be just and fear not" was John Bright's favorite motto, and as an abolitionist his eloquent speeches in Parliament served to promote Britain's abhorrence to slavery. Yet, his pacifism had limits, and he became the most forceful English supporter of the North during the American Civil War. It was John Bright's strive for peace and social justice that I later inherited.

My grandpa died of lung cancer when I was fourteen; my mother said that after he died, he had a look of wonderful peace on his face. I knew that God had taken this great man, and I wished that I had gotten to know him more because I had so many questions for him about his life working in the coal mines in Wales and his knowledge of John Bright.

4

WAKING UP TO GOD'S WORDS

THE FIRST TIME I distinctly heard God's words was the day after my eleventh birthday. I went to visit a friend nearby and was thinking that I would go through her backyard and have a quick climb on her makeshift monkey bar, before knocking on her backdoor. It was a set of pipes welded together so we could hang by our knees and generally fool around on. As I approached the monkey bars, I distinctly heard the words,

"It is time to put away childish things."

When I grabbed the bar I felt all the excitement and thrill of climbing rush out of me, and I just stood there. I never forgot the words or the feeling of change inside of me because I knew that it was time to grow up, whatever that meant.

The next year, when I turned twelve, I started to write poetry. God was seeking my attention on a daily basis. I became very serious about writing. Often I would spend time at the lake, found inspiration there, and then I would go home and work on my poems until late into the evening. I would write about nature and life but not about God, even though I was still the only family member attending church. I wrote throughout high school. After I had fallen asleep, or between 1:00 and

3:00 a.m., God woke me up so that I could write down the words that came into my head. If I did not write them down, I would have forgotten them.

It was so exciting to wake up with such creative ideas, but I often wondered where they came from because I was incapable of thinking of such wise and wonderful things. God's influence came to me unawares. Now, when He needs to give me a strong short message, He speaks to me seconds before waking me up.

One summer evening when I was nineteen, I was watching my parents drive away from the house for an evening outing, and I noticed the beautiful pink sunset in the sky and decided to dwell on it and on God's ability to create such beauty. I heard the words loud and clear in my mind,

"You will have a very difficult life."

I could not believe what I heard, and I felt a sickening dread in the pit of my stomach as I walked back into the house. I was determined to push the entire unbelievable experience as far back into my brain as possible. The following year, at the age of forty-four, my father began a new job as regional manager of Western Canada for a Swedish steel company. We were proud of him because he had worked so hard for twenty-five years to reach his goal. His new job included his own secretary and he would travel to Sweden and return home with fancy gifts. Within one year of starting his new job, my father noticed that his left hand was becoming paralyzed, and he was getting worse as the months went by. I had a foreboding sense that my entire life was going to fall apart.

My father's diagnosis was amyotrophic lateral sclerosis, known as ALS. Eventually he quit his job and I dropped out of college to help my mother take care of him at home. Over the next four years my mother and I watched him become completely paralyzed, while he saw himself slowly die, day by day. The doctors always gave us hope because a cure was being worked on, but hope was not a good thing because it never made my father better. It made us hang on to something that to us seemed like a lie. We did not want my father to die and neither did he. We would always talk about a cure, but it felt deceiving because we were all slowly dying inside, while he was dying outside.

I knew God loved me because I always felt His presence, and I expected Him to perform a miracle and heal my father because we all deserved it, and we had a lot of living left to do. God never did, and I felt God's ever-present love slowly drift away from me. I did not sleep much during those years and became so afraid of the dark and death that the entire experience devastated me. Suffering from so much trauma, I felt I was lost from God forever and would never find my way back.

No longer did the lake give me solace but instead a deep feeling of loneliness, so I stopped going there. After four years of illness, my father died of pneumonia at the age of forty-eight. His funeral was on my twenty-fourth birthday, and I thought that the whole scene was a lousy thing for God to do.

I could not feel any sense of comfort knowing that my father was with God, because I was not prepared to let my father go, ever. Nor was I able to reason as to why my father had died so young when we really needed him, and he needed us. The intense pain from grieving racked my body for years, and I stopped going to church. God stopped being a great and glorious mystery to me because He was nowhere to be found. Throughout my father's illness, my belief in God diminished day by day until I became separated from Him.

After his death, feeling utterly abandoned, and floundering for the next four years in darkness, I made wrong choices for myself because I was unable to feel God's direction in my life. Eventually I married and had a beautiful son. Two hours after my son was born, God's ever-loving presence returned to direct my life with a special purpose and show me many miracles, even to this day.

5

BIRTH OF MY SON

LEFT ALONE INSIDE my private room, I reflected on the miraculous birth of my son. I was feeling so honored in serving God in creating the miracle of a human life that it caused me to go way down, deep inside my heart. With reverence and gratitude, I touched the part of my heart that connected me to divinity and the part that God says, "I am in you." Instantly the room changed; before me stood a figure, which froze my heart. Its head was like a huge cloud of cotton, and in the center of its eyes burned brilliant orange flames. In absolute terror, I called upon Jesus, and Jesus answered. Immediately the horrific figure disappeared, and Jesus stood in front of me. He said,

"Never fear, I will always be near.
Do not be afraid,
I will never leave you and your son."

Jesus touched three fingers of my left hand and pressed them firmly down onto the bed. Feelings of bubbles went from His hand into my fingers and filled my entire body. He lingered for a few moments and then left.

The incredible sense of peace and assurance put me to sleep. I awoke a few hours later sensing that I had had a wonderful dream, until the recollection of His hand on mine sent me into a whirlwind, for His words never included my husband. I panicked, as I feared that I was going to raise my son alone.

Wondering what was going to happen to my husband, I foresaw a kind of death, and I was filled with a sense of dread. One year after our son was born, our marriage ended, and in my mind, I never imagined that this would ever happen.

Jesus knew this and appeared before me when my son was only two hours old. Many years later, I learned that Jesus had touched me with the Holy Spirit, God's Comforter, and through Him, I would receive the messages of God's amazing grace. From this grace, He wove within me a never-ending desire to seek and find goodness in all things. Often I saw His feet and the bottom of His garment as He walked beside me and my son.

6

GOD SPEAKING LOUD AND CLEAR

THE FIRST EXPERIENCE of hearing God's prophetic words was when I was preparing to leave for a five-hundred-mile journey by car to Vancouver, with a friend and my four-year old son. Prior to the trip, I had heard the works,

"Take up paper and pencil with you."

As soon as our journey began, I felt like the top of my head opened up, and words began pouring in. I wrote down the words as fast as I could. After reading them, I was amazed at their prophetic meaning. The message was for me, or so I thought.

"Love every day of your life and don't forget to love that life,
for it has nothing to do with winning or losing,
but rather what you make of it,
how you play the game.
The trials that one must encounter
do not necessarily have to be a burden,
but can be weightless and free from jogging the mind.
Depending on how you look at it,
your experiences can make you grow to heights

never known to mankind before.
So look to the light
and carry your torch with your fingertips,
and you will see a heavy world
change its shape and float away."

God was always close at hand; if I cleared my mind and gave Him my full attention, I could easily listen to His words and then write them down. It was as if someone was writing a great story in my ear, and I wrote with excitement. I thought that they were personal lessons, only for me. Always happy to receive them every morning, I knew they were going to help bring some coherence into my life. I learned from each one of them. Yet I still doubted my sanity and source of the words. I doubted all the time because I needed to be certain. Many times, I thought myself stressed out thinking I was hearing a voice, and I justified it to having a very creative imagination. I called it inspirational poetry.

The words came from me, but I was not the source. The messages were of a divine nature, guiding me and opening up my heart to God, His world, and everything in it. The birth of my son was the catalyst through which my life took a path directly toward God.

Often, as I saw the figure of Jesus walking with me, I believed that the voice I heard was His, but I was never sure. I tested myself after each message and was always full of doubts regarding the source. Surely, these words could not come from God. Truly, was God speaking to me? The uncertainty opened up my heart, and it took me twenty years to understand how God played a major role in my life.

"So, you are on your way to Vancouver.
What do you expect to do now?
Have you not bared your trials enough?
Let go, and let Me do it.
Think not of where you are going

but rather what you will do
when you reach that pinnacle.
Strip not your heart of love,
and I mean love for all.
Love everything and everything you do.
If it weren't for Me
you wouldn't be here,
and that, My child, is the truth,
all you need to know.
From where you sit look around you,
and look toward everything
with My light and My love."

7

MY INTERPRETATION OF GOD

I LEARNED THAT God is holy and loves us as we are, but we cannot commune directly with Him because we are not pure. Yet God always knows what is in our hearts and thoughts. God gave His Son, Jesus Christ, as a gift to all humanity, and through His death and the shedding of His blood, Jesus purified us by taking our mistakes and burying them forever. It was also His death that enables us when we die to be with God.

God's desire is for us to seek communion with Him. This is possible by speaking to His precious Son, Jesus Christ, who also taught us about the perfect love of God. To further and deepen a relationship with Jesus, it becomes necessary for us to be saved and baptized.

Once saved, our soul lives forever, and after death we can be with God. It is our deep desire to connect with God, and it is God's desire to commune with us. If we ask from our heart, Jesus will fill us with the Holy Spirit, a Comforter of a divine masculine presence, and through Him, we can commune with Jesus at any time, to request strength and healing and our daily needs. Jesus Christ and the Holy Spirit are separate, yet all are of God, and therefore, godly.

8

GOD LOVED US FIRST. THE FIRST MIRACLE

IN OUR DAILY lives, the center of our attention is not of God, because the details in our busy lives never focus on the presence of God. There are those of us who have never known that the reason we are able to love is because God loved us first. He started it all. This is the first miracle.

God gave His Son, Jesus Christ, to us, to be our friend and to teach us how to love. God taught us by example. According to God, the greatest sacrifice of love is to give up our life so that someone else may live. So God sacrificed His only Son, for everyone who lived in the world then and now, and when this greatest act of love was completed, Jesus returned to be with His Father. Prior to His departure from the world, Jesus promised that He would always be with us, and so He gave the world the Holy Spirit, a Comforter who speaks to our hearts. How can we not be in honor of this? How is it possible that the world is not aware of this great act of love? While God's Comforter is embracing us and speaking to our hearts, are we looking the other way and thinking about things of an ungodly nature?

"Like the hands of a clock
moving with time,

your heart knows
just what to do.
Your center is your perfect guide.
Always listen to these desires,
and you will be tuned into
the pulsing heartbeat of life itself."

God loved me so much that He sent His Comforter to speak to me every morning. His words were pillars of strength for me. He protected and guided my existence. He needed me to write down His words, and, unbeknownst to me, they were for everyone else. He constantly sought my attention and made me aware of His presence by performing small miracles.

On one occasion, my son was sitting in his stroller as we approached an intersection. The light signaled green, and the pedestrian sign signaled us to cross. An invisible wall prevented me from walking across, and I stood frozen staring at the green light. In a matter of seconds, a car out of control rounded the corner. The driver gained control and continued on, but would have hit us had we crossed the street. After the car passed in front of us, I came out of my frozen state. I saw Jesus's sandals and the bottom of His garment as He walked with us safely across the street.

On another occasion, when my son was three, we visited a playground, and he was attempting to climb to the top of the monkey bars. I watched in horror as he reached the top quickly. I could not climb up fast enough to grab him. He lost his grip and fell backward, his hands and feet pointed upward to the sky. He fell slowly, and it appeared that an invisible hand held him as it brought him gently to the ground. The hand released him, and he hit the bottom with a light thud. I climbed down and found him unhurt.

God is always seeking our attention. God was showing me that no matter what happened, He would always be there to catch us. How is it possible that the world is unaware of His magnificent presence, moment to moment and day by day?

"Yes, Carolle,
seek Me, and through Me
you shall find the true meaning of life.
Let not your heart be troubled,
if you believe in Me
you shall have everlasting life.
You remember I told you a long time ago
that you were My miracle?
Think not of your troubled life,
but count your blessings,
and choose your way of life
to be peaceful and restful,
free from doubts and shadows of your heart.
The times are changing,
and you shall see your spirit rise.
Go forth into the world and into your life,
with My blessings, My love, and My light."

9

WE ARE NEVER ALONE. THE SECOND MIRACLE

AT TIMES, LIFE can be difficult, and our concerns may be great, bogging us down with details. Meeting our needs can be such a struggle that sometime it appears that we may never meet them. Often it is necessary that, while sojourning, we must shift into another gear to maintain the high level of output our life demands from us. Sometimes we must do things alone; at least, that is what we feel during those harried times, but we are never alone. This is the second miracle.

"Well, child, here we go again
carousing every hill and every valley
wondering what is to come next, what is to be.
Have I ever told you how much I love you?
Think.
Your child I gave to you with My blessings.
Your troubles have nary stayed but drifted away.
That was all My doing, you know.
Yes, you have counted your blessings,
I never doubted that.
But you must change your life.
It is too complex for you, now.

Make it simple,
keep in harmony with those around you.
I will always be there when you need Me.
I am that small, still voice you hear within."

There may be times, when the struggle is too much for our soul, and it seems that our support system can no longer supply the nourishment to help us.

"Rest, be at peace.
I am always with you.
Try not to burden yourself with such a heavy load.
If you believe in Me,
you shall conquer over all things."

One winter, an elderly neighbor fell and broke her hip. I offered to help her out and take care of her cat. Her poor cat was very old and confused that her mistress was gone. My neighbor was in the hospital for six weeks, and I visited her as often as I could. Her only family lived far away, unable to see her. So I cleaned her house and visited her cat, Funny Face, until she was well enough to return home.

While in the hospital, she offered to pay me, but my heart emphatically said no. I knew she was having financial problems as well as being in great physical pain from her injury, and I could not imagine taking anything from her. I was also having financial problems and had become very distraught about my own personal situation.

One month later, I was babysitting a three-year-old boy, and since he only lived a few blocks from my house, I decided we should come to my place for lunch. He was excited about coming to Carolle's house and looking forward to visiting my three cats. When I picked him up, he was wearing his new summer hat, his spring coat, and a small Winnie the Pooh backpack. He looked so cute as we walked to my house holding hands together and looking at the new buds on the small bushes along the way. It was March, and the smell of spring was in the air.

When we reached my house, we went straight to the backyard. He walked in front of me because it was a narrow sidewalk between the two houses around to the back. I told him to wait by the backdoor so I could go in first and turn the light on. He said okay and stood there.

A split second passed between us; we stared at each other, and I felt that it was only yesterday I first met him when he was a beautiful baby. Now wearing his big summer hat, he had grown into a charming little boy.

I went inside my apartment, and instantly he was beside me. However, when I looked down at him, the top of his head went blurry. I squinted and blinked my eyes, and in disbelief I saw that his hat was gone from his head. I asked him where his hat was, and he looked up at me quizzically. Then he walked over to pat my cats. I looked everywhere for that hat but could not find it. I became extremely confused and distraught. How could I tell his parents that I had lost his new summer hat?

I decided to reorganize my thinking and dismissed the problem with the hat. So we had our little lunch, played for a few hours, and then left to return to his house. Since there was no other explanation, I concluded that the hat was only missing, and the question was "How had the hat disappeared from his head?"

This added more to my confusion and all my other worries. I was beside myself and could not imagine what I was going to say to his parents. We had just begun our trek home, and I was so anxious about the disappearing hat that I became sick to my stomach. Full of fear, the entire situation seemed unbelievable to me. In total terror, and feeling defeated, I gave in and asked God why the hat had disappeared. Instantly I heard the words,

"You are not focusing enough on Me and My presence."

I felt a great sense of peace overwhelm me, and I gave thanks for it. A few feet ahead of us was my little friend's hat laying on the ground close to the front steps of a tiny house across the street from where I lived. We stared at the hat all crumpled up in a heap, and he said, "Why is my hat on the floor?" I picked it up, smoothed it out, and said softly to myself, "You, my little friend, have just witnessed a miracle, and God is a never-ending solution to all problems."

My neighbor had become well, and her financial situation had straightened itself out. One morning she called me over and presented me with a substantial amount of money for all the work I had done for her. It was more than she had originally offered me. My heart was grateful, and it was enough to resolve my own financial situation.

The solution had always been there but I had become so engulfed in fear that I had lost faith and confidence that things were working out in my favor. My life seemed out of control. Appearances can be very deceiving. As long as we focus on God's goodness and grace and ask for what we need, He will always come through, no matter what. That is what He promised, and He is always true to His word.

God was seeking my attention and letting me know that it was the right thing to do by not accepting my neighbor's first gift of money. The Holy Spirit had spoken to my heart at that time, and I had listened. The disappearing hat had created total panic and confusion, and I felt disconcerted about my personal problems. I had stopped focusing on God. Instead, my entire body filled with dread and terror. Knowing I was helpless and defeated, I turned back to God and asked for His help, and He blessed me with peace and assurance, a flying hat, and paid-up debts.

"Be still, child, be still.
You are confronted with too much.
You cannot handle it without Me;
it is useless to try.

Just let go and let Me do it.
You are off balance today.
Do not do more than you can.
Try to relax.
Be steadfast in your faith;
I shall always be there with you.
By and by, all shall be revealed to you.
Just let things be, by leaving them alone.
I send you My light to shine with,
My love to be glad all over.
Things are not simple for you
because you are making them complex.
Branch out.
You must change your life.
The change will be good for you,
and leave Me the rest.
So be at peace, My child."

10

GOD'S COMFORTER GUIDES US. THE THIRD MIRACLE

THE QUESTION REMAINS, "How do we find God?" The answer is closer than we can imagine for the first step in finding God is through knowing His Son, Jesus Christ. There is nothing in the world that can separate us from the love of God, which is in Jesus Christ. There are times when we may turn from Him, but He is always there. Through Jesus, God sends us His Comforter to dwell in us and guide and direct us onto the right path. This is the third miracle.

Have you ever heard your heart speak? We all have a heart for God; we just do not focus on it. Instead, we tend to spend our time inside our minds.

"Today is a day of many wonders.
Listen with your heart to all things around you.
Look up past the skies to My direction.
Always in My care, I hold you.
Ever hold Me in your heart."

How do we let God help us? What do we do to make this idea work? It is not possible to give a problem to God. This does not make any sense. Is it possible that we can give a burden to God with, "You take care of it;

I can't do it!" This is too easy because life is too hard. "If I can't solve my situation, how can God?" "Is there a God?" "Where is God?"

"In everything there is a center.
As your universe revolves around the sun,
My world revolves around Me.
I am everywhere, in everything, and around all.
Man's heart is his center within,
but he has forgotten that his heart represents
an eternal force of Myself.
Look to your heart and follow these desires.
for they are of Me, a true perfection,
and carry hope, peace, and beauty.
Wake up your heart and live in it,
and you shall see your dreams
slip into reality."

Listen to your heart. Feel your heart and start speaking to it. If you are experiencing pain, then look inside and define it. If you are agonizing, then you can be sure that God knows your pain. God always knows what is in your heart. You will be speaking to God at the same time.

Perhaps you feel that because you are in so much pain you cannot feel God's presence. If God is unreachable inside of you, then you will have to find God outside, so look around at the beauty and power of nature, and then look upward.

"Like the cottonwoods,
climb upward to the sky,
Never stop loving Me,
that is all I ask."

"Have you ever stood on top of a mountain
and written down all there is to see?

You would have to stand there forever.
Your pen would never leave the page,
even in one lifetime,
for once you notice one beauty,
all the rest follows.
As in My world to follow,
your eyes will continue to find My beauty
in all things around you.
Have not I told you My kingdom shall come?
It is so near.
My blessings shall touch each and every one of you
who wish to help Me rebuild this earth.
Keep ever close to Me, Carolle, and your heart shall rise;
Your energy shall be reborn in the new.
Always be by My side.
Just as you witnessed last night
the old leaf exchanging itself for the new one,
you will eventually do the like.
My heart is ever with those
who remain to hear that small still voice within.
A new world is at hand;
help Me, My children."

11

GOD'S PROMISE. THE FOURTH MIRACLE

HOW CAN WE love God when our life is without love? Then simply remember that God will always love you, even when it seems that no one else will. His promise to you is one of everlasting love and mercy. This is the fourth miracle.

"Well, My child, here we go again.
Once more you will have to look to the light.
It will be difficult the next few days ahead.
But if you bear with Me, you shall see My wonders,
and they will never cease to amaze you.
Have a light heart; My love will never leave you."

When you finally realize this and begin to feel it, the impact will slowly change your life.

"Look to the sky, My light, My love,
grow upward with the trees,
and when you reach the top,
you will endure.
Your limits will prove to be boundless.

My love and My light
will shine inward and touch you,
and you will never be the same again."

You will understand your agonizing heart and want to heal the pain to make room for a real, true love, the love of Jesus Christ. He will send to you, straight to your heart, the Holy Spirit, God's Comforter, for direction in your daily life.

"In your times of trouble, seek Me,
and through Me your life shall shine."

How do we know that this is the Holy Spirit speaking and not our own mind?

"In the solitude of time, one can wake up and listen
to some of the events around him.
It's not much to listen to anymore,
especially to all that is happening.
We cannot exist by simply listening.
Listening with the mind and the heart
are two different ways to hear mankind.
One way with the mind, we simply do what we wish,
but with the heart we ponder over and over again
whether this or that is the right thing.
Nowadays, we are supposed to listen with the mind,
for the heart runs amuck.
It seems to be that all the muck around has been created
because one essential item was missing,
that being the heart.
For what if the hearts of men cannot see what is to be?
If they follow their minds,
watch them trip over obstacles,

which are burdensome.
The heart can rule the world,
and what a far better place it would be.
So why not try it.
Hope springs eternal in the minds of mankind.
Can you grasp that?
What is meant is that dreams exist in the mind,
but it is the heart that can rule the mind, creating miracles,
and miracles belong to each and every one of us.
Clear up your thoughts and mark your way in life
by creating a real world
born from the heart."

12

TUNE INTO YOUR HEART. THE FIFTH MIRACLE

REST ASSURED THERE are times when it is not possible to tune into everything around you. Life can feel so chaotic that we get caught up in our own ungodly thoughts. This is when it is necessary to tune into your heart, for your heart always knows what to do, no matter what the situation is. This is the fifth miracle.

"Certain things and events are important in your life.
You must remember them
and understand their hidden meanings.
It is not in spite, that you refuse to see the wonders;
you have simply chosen to ignore the lessons.
Your eyes are blind; your ears cannot hear,
and most of all,
your heart has ceased functioning its rightful way.
You must listen with your heart,
and feel with every sense of your being.
Create this world born from your heart,
the rightful heart,
the one being and remaining
the eternal force of your own creation.

Your center is clear and perfect.
Swim in it always,
and your eyes, ears, and body
shall cease the utter nonsense
it has created for itself."

Sometimes troubles are not of our own doing. They come bursting into our lives like a tidal wave washing over us. Any day is full of trials that we do not foresee. We anticipate, or at least hope, that the day will go smoothly. We never know what the day may bring or what gifts people may give to us, some good and others not so good. Although we may be able to handle situations, dubiousness can set in, creating self-doubts about our lives. Where do we go from here when we are stuck? We need the key to unlock the door.

"Look straight ahead and mind not the bitter trials.
They are only necessary for the next vital step
toward your spiritual growth.
The minds of men need never cease to dream for one second.
While hardships are encountered,
My light is always there.
Look for it, and cease your heartache;
happiness shall conquer all.
Stay in tune with all that is happening,
and never look away from the lessons.
Test your memory sometimes.
Remember all the joy you had,
and think of all the joy you have now."

13

YOU ARE GOD'S MIRACLE. THE SIXTH MIRACLE

IF YOU ARE thinking that you cannot remember experiencing any joy in your life, then it is essential to look backward and start from the beginning. You were born and are still here, alive and kicking. If you are unhappy, then look in the mirror and remember you are made in the image of God. That is the point. If you detest your image, then you must search inward and discover from where this idea originated. The moment you were born, you will always remain God's miracle. This is the sixth miracle.

"Child, remember your life is like a candle.
The flame flickers, wavers, and stands still.
In the end, the flame is snuffed out;
the light disappears, and that which is left
represents that death.
The candle that shone before has changed its form.
As in life and in death,
our spirit remains, and our body changes form.
Matter cannot be destroyed,
but reshaped over an eternity.

As My love shines,
you are created and re-created,
in My image for all time."

Perhaps you do not feel like God's creation because you have suffered maltreatment from others. Very often in our lifetime, our needs are unmet, and we can suffer tremendously from it, even for the rest of our lives. Hearts do break, and there may be a time when living no longer appears attractive. We feel totally useless and worthless.

"When blackness pervades deep within,
your heart stands still.
Hardened by this act of stillness,
all senses refuse to be themselves.
Anger begs release
when anger itself only burns more frustration,
and the nonflow of sensitive being
creates the blackness felt within.
When does this circle end?
When it is broken.
Light, too, casts shadows,
shadows of a brighter kind."

In understanding your past, you can re-create the present image of yourself to be one of truth and value. No matter what has happened to you or what you have done, you are still a valuable person, and nothing can ever change that. You are precious in God's eyes, so become precious in your own eyes. If your past is too difficult to endure, then at least attempt to come to an understanding of it. This is the first step toward healing.

"In these dark hours,
remember Me."

"Rest, rest assured things are fine.
Do not be afraid of what lies ahead;
do not worry.
I have been with you the first day,
and I have appeared to you
the morning I gave to you your son.
Do not be afraid you must alter your beliefs for others.
That is not necessary.
Suffering is to be your enemy, not your friend.
Remember to listen to others
and turn to Me for final direction.
Your love is strong; keep it ever flowing.
Do not misuse it and give it away where it is not wanted.
Do not wish harm to those who taunt you,
or give them power.
Look My way always;
I am the Truth, the Light, and the Way, child."

14

BROKEN HEARTS CAN AND DO MEND. THE SEVENTH MIRACLE

HAVE YOU BEEN betrayed? Humanity betrays you, and not God, and at times it may be no fault of your own. It is your heart betrayed. Your trust and security squashed. You were not in a safe place where your heart was free from harm. A hurt heart can feel like death. Hearts are bruised, break in two, or can feel wrenched from your entire body. What a terrible thing to happen to you! The very essence of your being, damaged or scarred. So what can you do about it? Once again, turn to the healing, for broken hearts can and do mend. This is the seventh miracle.

"Think love, child, think love.
Hold onto Me and grasp onto your dreams.
Through Me your dreams shall come true,
more than you will ever know.
What you desire is blessed by Me,
and through Me, you will learn to know
what the consequences of your life shall be.
It is difficult now for you, I know.
But you shall be tested in countless ways.
Your spirit shall rise up

and you shall see God through Me.
Think love, child,
and through Me you shall find your rewards.
Onward as you go,
you shall rise up higher than you will ever know."

One of the greatest obstacles to healing is nonforgiveness. Nonforgiveness is a battle that rears its ugly head as rage. To keep the war going is to perpetuate the rage from the constant feelings of pain and fear, due to loss. It becomes a battle that crushes the heart, creating sorrow and anguish, only releasing the rage once again. It becomes a circle of relentless darkness, which can evolve through generations. Its essence is a living death, and its name is hate.

Hate comes from a wounded heart and requires little effort to perpetuate itself. A damaged heart is always seeking ways to rid itself of pain, to heal itself. Very often, the pain releases violently toward living things and those closest and dearest to us.

Release the hate that is the darkness of pain and fear, through the healing process of grief. Then ask God's Comforter to enter and heal your heart. It is the Spirit of God that seeks to heal you through your broken heart. The Holy Spirit cannot come to you uninvited. Neither can it reside in a place of darkness or contempt or fear.

How can we expect miracles or believe in them when we are full of fear? It is the fear that binds and chokes us, demonstrating itself through rage. Anger, frustration, and anxiety can squeeze the heart and smother it. This is a place unsafe for your heart. It is a place where your heart has become hardened and you have become separated from God.

"Well, My child, here we go again.
Once more, you will have to look to the light.
It will be difficult the next few days ahead.
But if you bear with Me, you shall see My wonders,

and they will never cease to amaze you.
Have a light heart,
My love will never leave you."

At the end of my street lived an elderly widowed Polish lady, Mary. Often, as I passed by on my way to university, Mary would be outside sitting on her porch, feeding the birds or sweeping the sidewalk. I always stopped to speak with her because I found her sweet and charming, and she loved God so much but carried around within her a strong sense of sadness. She complained about her aching heart, and she said it was because the doctor told her that her heart was too large for her body. I always assured her that God needed her big heart, to pray for others and care for the squirrels, birds, and raccoons. She always laughed at this idea, but I really meant it.

In her garage at the back of the house, she had me make a small home for the local stray cat to sleep in. She worried all year around that God's creatures never had enough to eat, but I knew that she was feeding her own aching heart. Her only child, a daughter married with a son, had become so unhappy with her life that she committed suicide, leaving behind a stricken eight-year-old boy who struggled without a mother.

Later, the father remarried but the tragic loss of his mother filled the boy with so much pain he contained his rage inside, and his behavior became problematic. Mary tried to help him, but he was lost inside himself. She prayed all the time for him and his mother.

Mary had turned her small living room into a bedroom. A small single bed was against the farthest wall, opposite the large living room window. From there she could view her sunny window, and beside it was a table on which stood the most beautiful ceramic statue of the Virgin Mary that I had ever seen. The Virgin Mary stood over a foot tall; her gown was white and draped with a blue robe. Placed on her slightly bowed head was a golden crown; her eyes were closed, and her hands were held in prayer. Around the table on the floor, Mary had placed many vases of flowers, mostly roses, some artificial and some real. To the right of the table on the next wall was a fireplace, and on the mantel stood pictures of her daughter, family, and Jesus.

Mary never stopped praying. She prayed noon and night and went to church every day. She had a gold rosary draped around the Virgin Mary's neck, and at night, in the darkness of her room, she had noticed that a small medallion near the heart had begun to shine like a beacon.

She was very adamant about this, and I believed her. She also told me that she was having a prayer meeting in her home so she could receive some healing. She had invited a friend from the States to come, and she was so excited because he was well-known for his healing abilities. Mary knew that God was going to heal her physical body.

Her friend arrived, and the small room filled with people, overflowing into the hall, which led to the small kitchen at the back of the house. Everyone had brought food. For over an hour, I listened to this man talk about two specific people in the room who apparently were suffering greatly, emotionally. But he never mentioned Mary's troubles. To me, Mary had more physical and emotional struggles than what I was hearing. I examined him closely and hoped from his heart that he would feel Mary's intense pain. By this time, the aroma from the kitchen and the food simmering on the stove was so powerful that it was hard to concentrate on anything else, and I knew that he must have been hungry for it had been a long day. So he stopped talking and began praying over each one of us.

I was the only non-Catholic there and the only woman who did not wear a headscarf, but I still clutched my plastic pink rosary, given to me by a friend. I knew what the rosary represented, and I kept it tucked away as a small treasure believing that someday I would need it. Well, this was the time, and when it was my turn to receive prayer, clutching the rosary, I stared into his eyes wondering what he was thinking. I never did find out, but he did give me a short prayer, for which I was grateful. Finally, the prayers ended, the smell of Polish food simmering in the kitchen was overwhelming, and he said that it was time for lunch.

Everyone went to the kitchen except for Mary. I came back and sat beside her, and she was very sad. I did not ask her why because I already knew that she was still suffering in deep anguish with no relief. I asked her if she wanted some lunch, and she refused, so I went back to the kitchen and ate a little, and then I heard Mary call my name. The most amazing miracle was happening in Mary's living room, while everyone was eating in the kitchen.

The statue of the Virgin Mary was weeping oil from the bottom of her closed eyes down over her garments, disappearing before it hit the table. The oil simply vanished at the bottom edge of her garment, leaving her bare feet completely dry. I knew it was oil, fine oil, because it glistened as it gently and slowly seeped downward, in miniature tides.

I wanted to touch it but could not; instead I kneeled and stayed there for a while. No one came into the room; they were all busy eating and talking and had no clue what was really happening in Mary's living room. My brain went blank, and, without thinking, I got up, said good-bye to her, and went home to pray.

I needed to be alone because what I had seen was unbelievable. When I phoned later that day, Mary said the statue wept all afternoon and then ceased. A few years later, Mary died, and I knew she was finally with her daughter and Jesus.

One Sunday, while leaving the church around the corner from Mary's house, I met an older blind man waiting outside for a friend. Casually I asked him if he needed help to the subway, and he accepted my offer, and we began talking. He said he was from India and had assisted Mother Teresa start her Missionaries of Charity Order, which helped the destitute and dying in Calcutta. I found his stories fascinating and was sorry that I could not spend more time talking with him about his experiences with Mother Teresa, but my day was filled with unfinished tasks.

As I guided him to the subway, we passed Mary's house, and I told him about the miracle of the statue of the Virgin Mary. He wanted to know where the statue was, and I told him that I did not know, and I was not concerned, for statues do not weep. The miracle was not about the statue, but about the presence of God's anguish for Mary, and He felt her pain. God had wept, through the statue of the Virgin Mary, for Mary that day.

"Dear Carolle,
My child, My child,
do not forsake Me.
Do not disbelieve in Me.
I am yours now and forever more.
Look to My light always, My child.
Bear not your sorrows;
they are well away from you, now.
You shall shine in your glory.
You shall see Me.
Be not afraid;
take your time and follow my footsteps.
The path is well trodden
by others before you.
Look to Me and always
keep your eye on the straight and narrow path.
My light, My love,
I send to you always.
I am that small still voice you hear within.
Stay with Me,
and I shall remain with you for all eternity."

15

YOU ARE MASTER OF YOUR SPIRIT. THE EIGHTH MIRACLE

FIRST, YOU MUST be in a safe place to grieve and heal. If you cannot find a safe place, then ask for help in searching for good places and people who will support you in your grieving. If you are not in the position to find help, then look into your heart, body, and soul, and reach for the highest point possible, a place of goodness, of spirit.

If you have lost the connection to your own spirit, then reconnect to where you came from before you were born. Not from your mother or father, but from a higher place in which you cannot deny that you were born to be part of something greater than what you have become now. Imagine it! The greatest and highest point of your being is your spirit, light untouched. God and you are the master of this light. This is the eighth miracle.

"There comes a time when decisions are made
from each man's heart.
It is a lovely time, for he is blessed
with his heart's desire,
and within himself is a shining burning candle.
The flame is his spirit,

the candle his faith,
and the holder his love, which keeps it bound.
He is the master of this light,
for no man can touch it ever.
Remember to shine from within
and create your own world from without.
You are each separate, one from the other,
each with a different task at hand.
So go forth each day, and color your world
with the shining brightness that you are."

"I am your light.
You are My love.
I give to you, and you give to Me.
We share an never-ceasing love.
Hand in hand, My arm in yours,
together we can change the world.
What if the hearts of men are bogged down?
You can change this as long as you let Me show you the way.
This is a changing world;
a new world is forthcoming.
Don't let things upset you.
Let Me show you the way,
always,
My love, My life, and My light."

16

YOUR HEART COMMUNES WITH GOD. THE NINTH MIRACLE

IF YOU ARE having a difficult time finding help to change your situation, then you must never, never give up, because you are precious and deserve the very best from life. If you cannot change the situation, then seek refuge away from it from time to time. Your heart knows what to do. Listen to it, as it belongs to you. It is also where Jesus seeks communion with you through God's Comforter. Jesus knows what you feel and need, and He seeks to renew your heart to commune with God. This is the ninth miracle.

"My dear child,
wonders will never cease.
Look to My light, dear heart.
Look to Me always.
You are in My grasp, My arms ever clinging.
Your dark days are on you, well upon you.
Never cease loving Me,
and you shall see your darkness fade away."

"You are wayward at times.
You falter and stumble down into the deep wayside.
Let not your heart be troubled.
Leave it up to Me.
Have not I told you this over and over again?
Must I repeat Myself time and time again?
Believe in Me, and let your heart rise upward.
Go out today in My love and with My blessing."

17

YOU ARE ALWAYS WITH GOD. THE TENTH MIRACLE

THEREFORE, YOU MUST protect your heart, and if God knows what is in your heart at all times, then you are never alone. You are never without God, and nothing can ever change this. This is the tenth miracle.

If you are in an unsafe place or fighting for your life, then anxiety may be speaking to your heart through your stomach with feelings of fear. You may have tolerated these emotions all your life, and you may know nothing else. Perhaps you never imagined the possibility for change, as you have no control over the situation. Is it the fault of others? Blame and criticism cannot change people.

"Man's will to exist has still not freed him.
Afraid of so many things,
he walks the face of the earth
begrudging everyone in his way.
There are grits in his eyes and rocks in his way,
solid and massive things
obliterating his goals and shattering his dreams.
Mark your way in time, and you will see love's surrender."

Ask yourself what your heart needs. The answer may be in the need to be honored, so seek help to leave your present situation. Begin to make a safe place and use strategies to finalize the necessary changes. You need to have a sanctuary to call your own.

"A rose does not grip onto its own birth,
but frees itself from the obstacle of surviving.
It simply breaks free and lives,
and if not for this, then what should it do?
Don't live your life afraid; simply live it.
You owe it to yourself."

However, if you are unable to make a decision for fear that it will be wrong, look to your heart. Listen to it, and you will softly hear the right decision. Listening with your heart may be a problem with a damaged heart filled with too much pain. Perhaps you do not feel that you have a heart but only an emptiness full of blackness and despair. Perhaps it is enough for you to wake up and breathe, to try and get through another day, let alone have the energy to face your heart and listen to it.

"It takes courage to try something new;
it always has, and always will.
Why keep making yourself sick with old habit?
Advance into the new
and see the wonders it shall bring.
Only good will come of it all.
Give yourself a chance,
and you shall see wonders you could not possibly imagine.
I must repeat Myself;
you will continuously remain ill,
and your growth shall be stunted lest you change now,
not tomorrow, but now.
It is true change can be made gradual,

but in the end, the suffering is longer.
Do it now, and you shall see!
You remain with Me always."

Then, keep in mind, change will not occur if the start of change is not attempted. We are not meant to be stale but grow in spirituality.

"Well, there is much to do, Carolle, much to do.
You know that change must come about
if you expect to grow,
and one cannot grow unless one changes clothes,
lest he choke to death or remain stunted."

Remember that your heart needs a place of rest
with peace of mind and peace of soul.
"Rest your soul.
Rest your mind.
This is rest time."

18

GOD OPENS DOORS FOR YOU. THE ELEVENTH MIRACLE

EVEN IF YOU have no strength or hope left, perseverance is the key that will unlock the door to protecting your heart. Be smart and use discretion and discernment. God will open doors in such miraculous ways. This is the eleventh miracle.

"Look to this day,
for unto it is born a blessing.
A new day is here at hand,
and belongs to each and every one of you."

I love potato salad but seldom make it because of that reason. It is just too darn tasty, and my willpower is weak. So once in a while I make a bowl and treat myself, relishing every tasty morsel.

I opened up my cutlery drawer, and, lo and behold, I could not find my potato peeler. For the next few days I looked everywhere for it. I concluded that I must have accidentally thrown it out. So I ordered a new, fancy one from a Home and Kitchen catalog, and I had to wait for the potato salad.

My new potato peeler arrived, and it was terrific—better than the old one. Peeling potatoes was like peeling butter. I used it once, washed it, and put it away in its usual place. The next time I went to find it, it was not there. I knew I did not throw it out, and, once again, I looked all over for it. Perhaps I had become so absent-minded that it was stored somewhere it should not have been. Maybe if I found it I would also find the first peeler too. I looked everywhere I could imagine, but it was gone. Then I sat down and did some critical thinking. What if my first peeler had not been discarded, and where on earth would the second peeler be? Was God seeking my attention again? So I tuned into my heart and asked Him, and He answered,

"I am peeling away the old life
of malice, envy, greed, and hate."

I knew God was not referring to the problems in my personal life, but to another situation, which involved dissension within a group of people in our community. I was very preoccupied about this serious situation and felt saddened, rather than focusing on the presence of God, praying, and asking him for guidance to change things.

So, God sought me out. He was telling me that he had things under control and not to worry. Eventually, all problems were sorted out; the dissension evaporated, and I ordered a third potato peeler, which remains in my drawer today. I never did find the other two peelers.

"My child, sit down, be calm, relax.
My words will always be here for you,
with My light and My love.
I have spoken to you before, My child,
but that was long ago.
Remember to believe in Me with all your heart.
By and by your past and future
shall be revealed to you.

You have My power in your hands.
I have bestowed My love onto and into you.
You are My creation.
You are what dreams are made of.
You are a vessel that carries in it,
Myself,
and from there you hold the power
to make every dream possible.
My world is in need of this love.
You and the others will help Me to fulfill this dream,
to make My heaven on this earth.
You are strong, and your strength shall grow.
Take care of yourself.
I am in need of simplicity,
and peaceful minds and hearts.
Go now; My love always I give to you and yours."

19

WE ARE CREATED IN GOD'S IMAGE. THE TWELFTH MIRACLE

HOW DO WE let God take charge and help us, if we cannot find Him in our daily lives? Keep in mind that nothing can change the fact that we are created in His image. This is the twelfth miracle.

Can God get any closer to us than this? Should it not be our desire to see ourselves in His constant image of grace and affection? Should we not make our choices with this idea in mind? God cannot control the final choices that we make, for He can only direct us along the way. He wants us to seek Him out in our daily lives, to make good choices and benefit from them spiritually.

In a meditation, I saw a story. I was standing on a cloud and in front of me was an oak door, and flanked on each side stood a guardian angel. From my left, a single line of men approached me wearing long white robes. The line was endless, and each man represented a different culture.

I thought it strange and wondered where they were coming from until I realized they were returning home. The first man smiled and bowed to greet me and then moved on. I welcomed everyone, and time seemed endless until the last man had passed by, and the oak door opened. Out stepped a man of royalty. Holding a curved silver sword in a filigreed sheath, with a crimson tassel hanging from its handle, he bowed his head and offered the gift to me. I took it and drew it from its casing. Tossing it upward, it twirled higher and higher, turning into a blinding light, finally disappearing from sight into the heavens. I heard: "Everything returns to God."

"Calm, be calm, My child.
Rest your weary self.
You needn't fight any longer;
you have Me and all the others
to help you along your road.
You shall be so fine soon enough.
Do not worry about trivia.
Remember the moment, and live for it.
Do it any way you find works best for you.
You need not linger on your present problems,
or the unsolved past problems.
They will sort themselves out soon enough.
Live for the moment; I give each one to you,
with My blessing.
Live your life, child, to the best of your ability,
and life will give back to you, all that you deserve.
This circle represents My love, which I give to all,
and in turn gives back to Me.
This circle, My love, envelopes you all;
as it was in the beginning, it remains
the same today and always forever more.
So be it, My child, life starts and ends with Me."

20

GOD ALWAYS FORGIVES US. THE THIRTEENTH MIRACLE

SO DOES IT not behoove us to honor God more in our lives by looking around and finding His presence? If we cannot hear God's Spirit in our hearts, the fact remains that God will never let us down, because of His promise of love and forgiveness. God needs our relationship with Him and loves us, unconditionally. He will always forgive us if we ask and bury our mistakes and never remember them again. This is the thirteenth miracle.

"Dear child, do not ever leave Me.
I have loved you since the day you were born.
It is not I that is drifting away from you,
it is you drifting from Me.
Keep ever close to Me.
Think not often of those who have done you wrong,
but rather think of Me and all there is of Me.
Do not grasp in the darkness
for something that will do you no good.
Come to Me always in the light,
where you will find My love also, always.
Keep ever close to Me, and watch the darkness elude itself."

"Don't be discouraged, child.
You have struggled much in your lifetime.
Sincerely you have naught to worry;
yours is all healed, the suffering over.
Your strength has carried you far.
You need naught to worry about this.
What is required of you now is simply patience
and fortitude to control your emotions.
Do not, I repeat, do not, let things upset you easily.
That is one thing you must work on.
Be kind, be patient, and trod slowly.
Look around you always, and constantly
be aware of Me.
That is all I ask of thee.
Be at peace.
Be calm, and be still, just as the clouds
move slowly along your road.
Things are still waiting to be revealed to you.
By and by, you shall see My wonders
shine through you.
Never fear; I shall always be near."

21

LONELINESS AND DEPRESSION. THE FOURTEENTH MIRACLE

PART OF GOD'S covenant is to love us, no matter what. The reason God wishes us to know this is to save us from harming ourselves and others. The more we attempt to understand this, our relationship with God becomes deeper. God loves us so much and wants us to continue to seek Him out. This is the fourteenth miracle.

"You underestimate yourself.
That is Me you are underestimating.
With all that I have shown you,
you still refuse to believe.
Let go and let Me do it all."

If there is a life of sheer beauty that you cannot see for yourself, then see it in the lives of others. This means that by deductive reasoning, if others have a life of goodness and decency, which you desire, then you deserve the same experiences no matter what your loss. Can you grasp that?

"The birds and the clouds,
together they fly.
They ask naught but know they are blessed;

like them, you are.
Look My way, and you shall always
remain full and happy."

What does one do when in a deep depression? Deep depression can be caused by a myriad of feelings such as being let down, offended, or even betrayed. It can develop from a situation we are not responsible for but affected by, or perhaps one we have totally created for ourselves. That is the impact felt when we can no longer handle the situation. Our strength is sapped; we have no fortress to run to.

The complex situation will not go away, but instead it may take a unique turn for the worse, if we have no means to change things because solutions appear to be so far away. We desire to leave the situation by withdrawal or addictions; it is because we cannot foster a quick remedy to ease the pain. Darkness can result and permeate our entire existence.

"What would you do
if you were alone with nothing alive around you?
You would simply die in all that darkness.
My love keeps your body alive,
and My light clears the darkness,
and lets you look beyond."

Loneliness is the accompaniment to living in hell. Loneliness creates the darkness and lack of breath. Loneliness can be the separation from life, the part of you that connects to the totality of everything alive. To be cut off is a very dangerous thing. Life is so precious. It is sad and painful when a life dies, be it a person or creature. In our hearts, we feel the utter loss because we cannot alter the situation.

God is the creator of all life. We cannot give life, so we have no right to take our own life. To get away from fear, panic, and destruction is to think how God would think and not how men would think. God made us the partakers, in life and it is our purpose to help life along and keep it going. You cannot serve two masters, God and the other stuff.

In a meditation I saw a story. I stood on a cloud and could see the earth beneath me. To my right stood an oak door, and standing in front of me was Jesus, His right hand was raised and in His left hand, He held a lantern. Passing it to me, He said,

"Spread the light to others,
which you are,
and follow Me."

He turned and walked through the oak door, and following close behind Him was the population of humanity traveling downward to the earth.

"My dear child,
Wonders will never cease.
Look to My light, dear heart,
look to Me always.
You are in My grasp, My arms ever clinging.
Your dark days are on you,
well upon you.
Never cease loving Me
and you shall see your darkness fade away.
Hang on to your faith;
it is a light for others grasping in the darkness.
Your trials are hard to bear.
You have no choice but to bear them.
I have put you under a test so difficult
others would have ceased loving Me long ago.
Your love is true to Me,
and your faith
shall be used as a stepping stone
for others losing their step.

Your time is upon you now;
difficult days are still ahead.
But these are only numbered.
Look always to Me,
My light, My love, My child."

I knew a man who had suffered a great loss in his life. The person he loved the most had died of cancer, and he could not handle the loneliness, so he turned to drugs to kill his pain of loss. I could not believe how this man had changed and fell so far from grace, so I decided to rescue him and help him to get back onto his feet. After discussing the situation with him, he agreed to come back to his senses.

I took him out for something to eat, since he had become very frail while living on drugs. After the meal was finished, we returned to his sixth-floor apartment; he went straight to bed and fell into a deep sleep. I spent the next four hours cleaning and doing five loads of laundry. The place had little furniture in it and no telephone, but there was a new and fancy twenty-speed bike on the balcony. I suspected that the owner would come to reclaim it, since word was out that the apartment was no longer a place to deal drugs.

Later in the evening, my friend was out cold in a very deep sleep, and I could not stir him. I knew he would sleep well into the morning. There was a knock on the door, and looking through the peephole, I saw a very large man demanding his bike. I told him that I would give it to him if he stood at the end of the hall. He refused to do this, so I had to think about what to do next.

Feeling unsafe, I could not call anyone for help because there was no telephone. The other tenants did not come out to see what the commotion was all about, since they were used to the drug scene across the hall, and so they ignored it.

I knew I had to remedy this situation quickly because I had to work the next morning and needed a good night's sleep. Since there was no one to come to my rescue, I became extremely fearful, and so I prayed. Calling upon God and Jesus, the Holy Spirit and Mother Mary, I also called down any other angelic being that I figured might be watching over me. I also asked for those heavenly guardians whom I did not know were watching over me, and then every angelic being that possibly existed in all of heaven, to help me. I prayed my heart out because I felt evil around me, and I knew I was in grave danger.

I was depending on this help and believed it was there when I opened the door to push the bike out. Not having enough time to move the bike out of the doorway, the man was almost on top of me with his fist raised high over his head. I knew he wanted to hurt me. For a split second, many thoughts went through my mind, and I was shocked as to why he would want to do this. I believed I was a nice person who worked hard to do good things and take care of my son. That was the first time I looked evil in the face and saw that in its eyes it had no conscience because it had no heart.

As the man stood in front of me with his raised fist, I pushed the bike with all my force. Although I knew he was stronger than I was, I had faith that God would mysteriously help me. My relationship with God was very strong, and I never doubted His love for me for one second. Then something marvelous happened, and I have never forgotten God's protection.

I saw a flashing white light in the shape of a sword come down between us. It hit the seat of the bike, throwing it and the man with such force he was lifted off his feet and thrown into the hall, against the wall, with the bike on top of him. I closed and locked the door, praised God, and then I went to bed and fell asleep. When I awoke the next morning I thought about God's miracle and the mystery of its appearance in absolute silence.

Two weeks later, my friend had succumbed back into his dark world because he had not wanted to change his life. It was too difficult for him to do alone, and I could not help him see the light that he was not alone, so I let him be. The sad thing was that God's light had revealed itself in his apartment, and he had missed it.

"Look to My light and keep to it.
In time you will know where you fit.
Leave it to Me.
I have a special place in this life
and a hearty plan
worked out for you.
You shall know your direction
and be free and weightless
from all cares.
I want you to slow down more.
Peace be with you and yours.
Rest your heart, be glad and thankful,
for all the wonders you have seen,
and those that remain with you, now."

22

PEACE OF MIND. THE FIFTEENTH MIRACLE

TO CLIMB OUT of hell, you must first make a decision to leave that place. No matter how weak and weary you are from being beaten down, it is possible to have peace of mind. This is the fifteenth miracle.

First, ask God for help, and then ask for help from those in places where you think you may receive it. Though you may feel doubtful and lack insight, continue seeking help in new and safe places. You will begin to receive it, for God always knows what is in your heart. He will always bless you and open a new door.

"Child, peace be with you, My love.
I have watched you closely over the past few weeks.
You are in desperate need of change,
and it is needed quickly.
It is needed now lest you may drift from Me.
You will be freed from all your past burdens.
They have carried you along your way.
You can let them fall free now
and look toward Me.
The light, which represents My love,

the torch, which you carry,
represents your faith in Me.
I give everyone a torch to bear;
some bear it;
some let it fall to the wayside,
and some simply ignore it, and it fades to a flicker.
The light is here for all of you
to light your darkness,
and to warm and keep your body alive.
You will begin to see wonders now.
The clouds will part, and the path beyond
shall reveal itself to you.
But remember, My love, My child,
be wary of those who taunt you
and say ill words about you.
Ignore it always.
There is nothing stronger in this world than love,
My love, and without it,
My world, which belongs to you,
shall pass and fade away."

So stay with that which only does you good, and keep giving up the ungodly stuff. Though the situation may be trying, you will learn to find safe places, and you will go through many changes. The world is full of deception and can be a hard and tricky place. Betrayal comes from people and not from God. If you blame God, then you will never get to know Him or see His miracles.

There is always hope, and there is always light. There are strategies you can follow if you do not yet have God in your life. Releasing ungodly things is the first step onto the path of decency, goodness, and grace.

"Be wary of those who taunt you
and make you ill at ease,
for their vibrations are confused,
and their mind is not true to their heart.
Darkness and confusion will administer their life.
Ignore this always,
and look to the brightness everywhere, thereof."

"Carolle, sweet child.
You must flow along with the wind.
Support is close at hand,
as I am always nearby watching and waiting for you
to surrender yourself in my direction.
Your needs are being met, dear child.
You talk often to yourself about your worries.
You know all these things will work out.
You must stay on top of things.
Keep in the habit of being aware of that which is around you,
and you will find your place in the wind."

At times, why are the lessons of life so difficult and troubling? Why does it seem that as the years go by, nothing seems to get better? The struggles increase and the question remains, "What is it all for if it is not working out for my sake?" If we cannot make it work, and no one can help us, then where do we go with our poverty and unhappiness? What do we do with it all?

Poverty

"Once it seems we have ventured over broken roads,
we've done it all before.
A passing day did not matter,
for we were left inside one room.
We did not care how late the day had come;
we only knew that after dark had just begun,
you would be standing at the door,
our father, so proud of you we are.
You need not care, if faces we are sad;
you've met it all before.
When you were young you lived this life too.

Take not what does not belong to you.
Give away that which you can afford.
Look to the heavens, for each day needs a miracle.
Only love can pull you all through this,
the cracked mire and dust ahead.

Problems we encounter need never stay but drift away.
The sad are born forlorn,
but they only wear masks,
for underneath is a golden world of hope.
By turning away from these depths of despair,
look toward the sun, and
a new world is at hand,
and will come down to your level.
It's not true we cannot afford these things,
nor do we not deserve them.
Look My way and watch it all change shape.

The world is yours and ever belongs to you,
so take it fully and make use of it from the heart.
A golden globe cannot exist,
without first a source of light.
Look to My light and take heed of it;
the future is yours and mightily belongs to you."

23

CONNECTED TO GOD AND THE UNIVERSE. THE SIXTEENTH MIRACLE

IF THERE ARE no solutions around, then it is time to look inside your heart, into the real depths of your being, and do some soul-searching into your spirituality. This is your connection to your Creator and to the whole universe. This is the sixteenth miracle.

"The sun rising and setting is like man's eternal journey.
Full of life, he must stand tall
and accept the ways along his chosen road.
At times, the path will be clear,
and at other times
full of chaos pushing him backward,
but only a few steps.
His life is actually faultless,
for where would he be without the lessons?
Yours is a love true to the earth.
You've accepted all you faced
and understood the consequences.
All lessons are a blessing in disguise.
Look for their hidden meaning,
and never stop loving life.

Grow with all that is around you,
and your spirit shall expand upward and outward."

"You must stop all manners of defiling yourself.
Look My way, and My words will ever follow you.
It matters what you are to Me,
and what you become
will eventually tell its own story.
But lest you stop all subordinating
and cease this foolishness,
My words will never flow past these pages,
and they will cease to become
a part of men's hearts.
There is a beauty lying within My words.
It is up to you to show this newness,
and stop all tilting of your bodily functions.
I cannot work with you while you are physically unfit;
cleanse yourself, and help Me reshape
this world of ours.
Finish all manners of waywardness,
and look to Me always.
My light is evermore and shall remain so for eternity."

24

GOD'S IMAGE OF PERFECT LOVE. THE SEVENTEENTH MIRACLE

THE PROMISE GOD made to us is one of pure love. Even though we may continue to make mistakes throughout our lives, God is watching and seeking our attention. No matter what we do, He continues to love us. So why should we not love ourselves? After all, God made us in His image of perfect love. This is the seventeenth miracle.

"Merge into one with all that is around you,
like My daughters the clouds, flowing in unison.
Never let go of all that you have,
look My way and behold My wonders.
Never stop the love flowing;
you that receive it are mightily blessed.
Send forth your love
and create a cloud of each other
merging together as one.
My love is all there is.
So billow forth, expand and grow,
until there is only Me you see."

"Yes, Carolle, seek Me, and through Me

you shall find the true meaning of life.
Let not your heart be troubled.
If ye believe in Me, ye shall have everlasting life.
You remember I told you a long time ago that
you were My miracle.
Think not of your troubled life
but count your blessings
and choose your way of life
to be peaceful and restful,
free from doubts and shadows of your heart.
The times are changing,
and you shall see your spirit rise.
Go forth into the world, into your life
with My blessings, My love, and My light."

25

LIFE IS FOR THE LIVING. THE EIGHTEENTH MIRACLE

PERHAPS YOU DO not see God in your own image, and perhaps you never have. Who knows what the image of God looks like anyhow! Have you forgotten or were you never told, that once created in God's image, nothing can ever change that, whether you want to believe it, or not? The fact remains that you are here because God made it so. This is the eighteenth miracle. You are part and parcel of the whole process of life, and life is for the living.

"The world is like the sun, round and full.
The energy it displays is not visible like the sun,
for were it visible, men would become blind.
Before they can see this wonderful cosmic force,
they must first change the world within themselves.
In every universe there is a center.
As the planets and stars revolve around the sun,
man's destinies and wishes revolve around his heart.
Be in harmony with everything around you.
Remember your center and evolve within yourself.
You, too, are part of all this creation.
Were it not for Me, all this would pass away.

Be part of all, and in part your destinies
and desires will rise in front of your eyes.
Your future you shall always know.
Follow always your heart, and everything,
everywhere will continue to grow in cosmic force."

We are born, and then we die. Do we only think of God when we witness birth and death? What about the part that exists in between these two miraculous events? Where is God during our lifetime? How often have we thought of Him? Does it amount to seconds and minutes, or have we never been aware or even felt His presence?

Take a look around; witness the power of nature, and connect it to yourself and others around you for we are of that nature, entwined and needing each other. We are children of the universe, God's universe. We need to take responsibility for our experiences and our relationship to the world.

Having accountability for our actions and how they affect others is always a step in the direction of righteousness. This word is rarely used in our daily speech. Righteousness connotes a sense of divine responsibility to ourselves, one another, and everything in the world.

"Take care of yourself;
these are priceless gifts
I give to you.
Your body is faultless.
Have courage and remain dignified always.
My life I give to you.
Remain exalted at all times."

With our gratitude, God will bless us, and His mercy is the healer. Gratitude is the path that leads you out of despair and onto the path of forgiveness. Forgiveness leads to grace and peace. You are God's workmanship and have been given a life.

"Look unto this day,
for each and every favor
bestowed onto you."

"Dear child,
Things are working out, aren't they?
Have I not told you this time and time again?
Simply have faith and let Me do it.
It is the hardest thing to do at times,
to simply let things be.
True, we are supposed to be masters of our fate,
but we have forgotten so often that we, too,
have a master, a spiritual guide, a sailor.
At this time in your life,
you are making a journey across water,
and this is referred to as a spiritual journey.
I am your guide and you shall ever trust Me
to lead you along the way.
The waters shall cease rising,
and the waves will calm, soon enough.
You have done well,
but it is vital you continue to think and act
in your best interests.
Only then shall the best in you shine forth,
and that, child, is a blessed thing.
You, in yourself, are My blessing.
I give each of you to My world.
Make the best of it and take the best in it.
Let no others prevent you from receiving

the good in life.
You are all here and are needed.
So remember, shine from within, look to Me always,
and your life will remain happy.
I give to you all My blessings of life and love.
Go with it now and cease living in a rut
you make for yourself.
Look to My light and go with it.
You have done well but shall do better.
By taking care of yourself, you are thanking Me.
Go now in peace.
I love you, My child."

Once we accept God into our lives, getting to know God is a process of examination and testing. The most important rule in having a relationship with God is to allow ourselves to admit to our deep feelings of insecurity and lack of faith. God is here to help us and always knows our needs.

"You must be at peace, Carolle.
You must rest your mind and heart.
All is well.
It is up to you to believe.
Have not I told you this, over and over?
Leave not your senses for one minute, or one second.
Look to Me, My way."

It is not possible to speak to God if our heart is not pure. So the first step is to honestly admit your imperfections and humbly admit defeat. You cannot make the right choices for yourself without God's direction in your life.

I had come to a point in my working career that I felt it was time to move on. I knew my purpose there was finishing up. I was unsure when I would be leaving, so I asked God for guidance. I had worn a new shirt and put it in the laundry, and when I went to wash it, it was not there. The shirt was part of the dress code of my present job, and I looked around to see if I had misplaced it, but I knew I had not. I searched throughout my bedroom and anywhere else it could have possibly been. Finally, I gave up because I knew that it was nowhere to be found. It was not uncommon for God to show me a miracle, to make a point.

I sat on the bed and pondered about the meaning of the situation. I knew God had taken the shirt. I finally asked Him why He had done this, and instantly He said,

"You no longer need it; you are moving on."

Shortly afterward, I did move on, and I never, ever, found the shirt.

"Child, sacred child,
all things are sacred to you too.
It is a blessed thing
to receive this gift of love from Me to you.
Go and sprinkle it forth.
Everywhere let this light of love shine.
You are My wonders, and I will repeat
My blessings onto you, time and time again.
Go now with My light, My love, and all
My blessings.
I give to you the gift of love,
which in itself represents the gift of life.
Go forth; go now.
That is all, My child.
My love and My life, forever more."

26

FORGIVENESS. THE NINETEENTH MIRACLE

ONE OF OUR greatest teachers is humiliation. Humility is the way in which we must approach God, whenever we need to speak to God. So go before God and ask for help when faced with grave consequences. Remember that forgiveness is the key in having your prayers answered. Forgive those who have harmed you, forgive yourself, and then ask God to do likewise. If you are not able to forgive, then ask God to deal with it. This is the nineteenth miracle.

"All I ask is that you let Me do it."

Without responsibility, there can be no forgiveness. Without forgiveness, there will be no serenity, and this is a block on the road to fulfillment. Bad things can happen, injuring the heart, the sense of loss and feelings of pain so intense that they can become consuming. God wants us to get closer to Him, but the loss can be so great that the rage becomes explosive. There will be no room in our heart for God's light if our heart is filled with darkness.

"Child, don't be terribly sad;
you have so much to look forward to later on.
You are going through an incredible emotional change.
Hang on to Me and to yourself.
Know you are loved by those who truly love you.
You are all having a hard time.
Your son is well and happy.
Cling on to the love that surrounds you;
only give of what you can afford.
Assert your needs to those around you.
Do not fight your situation;
it will straighten out itself.
Keep to the light and My love, child."

However, forgiveness may take years or never be possible, the tragedy and sense of loss too incomprehensible. If this is to be, then the step of having faith and assurance that things will work out may not be possible. The ache you feel inside is not of God but the intense separation from God. We ache not for separation but for healing. Loss is very painful, and that is the precise time in which we need to be filled with God's love and His healing. By focusing on forgiveness and asking God for help, the pain can leave, for God always forgives us if we ask Him to. Then should we not find it in our hearts to forgive others?

The trick is to be in control of the anger that pops up unexpectedly until the healing is complete. Constant forgiveness and asking God for strength is the key. For as long as it takes—days, months, or years—never be weary of doing this. The process will open up your heart, and the journey to fulfillment will be possible. If your burden is too great, then imagine yourself handing this painful bundle over to God, and let God deal with it.

"Well, watch the night roll by.
The clouds also do their share.
They are not locked in the hearts of men
but float freely in the sky at their own pace.
We shall not deliver a new earth,
a new peace,
a new peaceful way of living,
lest man changes his clothes, his attitudes.
Look to the sky always,
and see the freeness that shines forth.
The sun always remains,
sometimes hidden, sometimes not.
The rain falls sometimes long, sometimes not.
Man never shows himself black or white, but gray.
He should drop all manners of confusion
and throw away the grit he finds between his teeth.
Breathe deeper, and let the source of your life flow easier.
Look up to the sky and to the clouds,
up in My direction,
and change your face to what lies beyond.
Never fear; I am near, always.
Just look up and clean your vision
to really what lies in front of your eyes.
You, too, can have an endless life of sheer beauty
if you can only look past your attitudes, beliefs, and prejudices.
What matters is the sky, the clouds and the sun,
and when you finally see these things,
you will notice the hidden beauties
in those and everything around you."

27

YOU ARE MASTER OF YOUR HEART. THE TWENTIETH MIRACLE

ONCE FORGIVENESS IS achieved, you will receive serenity and a heart for God. God's Comforter, the Holy Spirit, will guide you through your entire life and show you amazing things. This is the twentieth miracle. The trick is to maintain a heart for God. You are the master of your own heart, where the Spirit of God dwells.

In a meditation, I saw a story. Before me stood a man draped in a soiled cloth, his hair unclean and his face unshaven. He grasped both hands within the sleeves of his long garment, which was tied loosely around his waist. I saw his eyes filled with great sadness, but it did nothing for my feelings of disdain for his smelly and shabby appearance. I asked him who he was, but he did not reply, instead he lowered his head in shame. I did not trust him and told him so. Still he did not answer. As I turned to walk away, I became overwhelmed with a sense of warmth and peace at my back, and turning around, I saw that the shabby man had turned into a glorious angel. Slowly it raised both hands, revealing, within its brilliant white heart, a golden flame. The angel's eyes burned into mine as it spoke:

"Love Me as I am,
for I am all souls.
I am your angel of mercy and guide of love."

"Carolle, dear child,
you have waited a long time to find Me,
to see Me.
With your love for Me, you shall see more
than only Me,
but will eventually see God.
Keep up your strength, and keep your faith.
You have served many masters but finally
are serving
the rightful one, Me.
Look to Me always, and I shall ever guide you,
for I am your true master.
Remember to discriminate your love.
Though you meet people who are floundering,
keep your business of Me close to you.
I shall guide you to release that God inside of you.
My voice is faint yet ever clear to you,
now and always.
Look My way, and you shall shine and see
wonders, My child.
That is all; good night, My dear child."

At the heart of God is great mercy and compassion. If you do not know what to surrender to, then surrender to the things that will do you good. What you need is love and peace of mind. So really search for these things in your life. Give up that which causes you unhappiness and seek that which is real and fulfilling.

"Man was not born to be in a rut,
but ever changing like the seasons.
There is a timing to all things,
to everything."

"Those lost years, it seems, are gone, forgotten.
Yet it is not time to let these things go.
No matter what you fear, I am near always.
Your mind has not made up exactly
just what to do.
Do not grasp in the darkness; come to Me in the light.
You have a heavy burden, you say?
Look at Me; come to Me always.
Have I not always shown you a safer door to go through
than the one you just left behind?
Your trials are behind you now.
You are afraid of the power of My words;
they are a blessing to you in disguise.
Just let it out.
You never feared Me when you were afraid
and needed Me, and I came to you then, as I do always.
Open up your heart, Carolle, it is dying to be let out;
only good can come forth.
You are making yourself sick not doing so.
Look to Me, and I will ever guide you.
Do not fear anything; all that is happening is good.
People need My words, so let them forth.
Spew them out, and they will never cease to flow."

28

HAPPINESS

TRUE HAPPINESS EXISTS from things of the spirit; without this spiritual connection to God and things godly, you will never know the true you. If ungodly things of the world have bruised your spirit, then remember that you can be in the world and still be true to your own heart.

"This is a house of love.
You are all gathered here in My light.
I send you My love;
enjoy it.
It is here for you."

Search for that which is real. Start with you. You are here; that is real, and go from there. You are a product of your past, past generations, and of your present environment. If you do not like the world that surrounds you, then change what you can and limit your relationship to it.

Surrender to your fragility and weaknesses. Your failures have consequences, so look at them. Surrender to your limitations, losses, heartaches, and broken dreams; roll them into a package and surrender them to God, for they are also His burdens. If you give them all up to God, He will make the necessary changes and compensate you for your losses. Surrender to your humility, humbleness, and have compassion for yourself, and then you are honoring God.

"Rise up;
rise up to the sky;
float to the top.
It's easy;
just let go."

Granted, life may be full of troubles, and at times, we may feel helpless. As long as we have a heart for God, we must continue to learn how to use it daily. As long as we listen, we can always find God's Spirit, inside our hearts. He will always guide us from that place within us. He knows our hearts and knows what we need, and, believe it or not, new doors will open.

"Blessed are the meek,
for they shall inherit the earth.
Blessed are the poor,
for they shall see God.

What you see, you shall receive.
Never refuse My wonders,
for without them you shall never be.
Your soul is blessed at the beginning
and carries within it all My love.
Look to Me always, and you shall see God.
Look to Me always, and your cup shall be filled.
Look always My way, and your life shall overflow.
Count your blessings.
They shall remain with you
as long as you hold Me in your hands.
Grasp onto your faith;
others need it also."

29

THINGS WILL ALL COME TOGETHER

SPRING WAS APPROACHING, and it is my favorite time of year. It is a time that sings of a new season of sunshine and warmth and a renewal of the spirit of life. Easter was also approaching, and I was reflecting on the first Easter story and the boundless love of God and how real it is. His constant desire for us to become holy always overwhelms me. I was also reflecting on my son's accomplishments and my book finally being completed.

My son had grown into a fine and happy young man and had achieved his dream of becoming a successful computer graphic animator. I was grateful for that, and I could not have helped him without God's presence in my life. My book, God's book, was almost finished, and I was happy for that too. However, I was living in another province and had become so homesick for my son and Toronto that I was heartsick.

To complicate matters further, I had a strange feeling that I was being lifted up, and that my time left on earth was shortening. The feeling had come upon me quickly and lasted for an entire week, throughout Easter. The sense of sadness depressed me, and I decided to talk to God about it. I told Him that I really did not want to go because I had too many things left to do. Then God showed me a miracle.

I was sitting on the couch in my living room in deep prayer with

God when I heard a sharp cracking sound come from my china cabinet. I looked over and saw that a new, tapered, unlit candle, sitting in a small square candleholder, had fallen, knocking over a picture of my son and his fiancée. When I picked up the candle to place it in its holder, I saw that the candleholder had split evenly down the middle, into two parts. The two halves were separated by one half inch of space as they sat on the shelf. Picking the pieces up, I checked to see if there had been a crack causing it to split apart, but there was none. As I placed the two pieces together, I questioned in my heart how this could possibly have happened, and I heard these words: "Things will all come together."

Instantly my depression left me, and I returned home three years later.

"Well, Carolle, things are working out.
You must be patient; the time is not right yet.
You must grasp on to everything you believe in.
It will be difficult
and seem extremely hard at times,
but never let go of Me.
I shall always be with you,
now and forever more; that is all."

30

GOD IS COMMITTED TO YOU

EVER SO SOFTLY, God's Comforter speaks to our hearts, and this is how He prays to us. By praying back, it is possible to establish a relationship and deep love for God. He knows our needs. Is this not fantastic?

Prayer is our connection to Jesus, and the higher our thoughts become, the more frequently He will call upon us, through the Holy Spirit. Speaking to Jesus through prayer is also the connection to our Creator. So, while we pray it is important to remember two things: we are divine because we are His workmanship and righteous because the Holy Spirit can dwell in us. Therefore, with this approach of reverence, we can receive healing in that which we need and eventually fulfillment in that which we seek. This is the path on which God allows us the freedom to search and find true spiritual happiness.

When you develop a deep love for God, Jesus will send you His Comforter. You will hear His words of wisdom, and He will speak to you daily, ever so softly. God's committed to you. Does He not deserve the same respect?

"Well, My child, My child,
think of Me,
all the time, often, always think of Me.

Think, think, think.
Do what you must, but do it of Me,
in My love.
Think of Me at will.
Think of Me all ways."

We need to love God, ourselves, and each other. As entwined as it is, this relationship is also connected with the relationship to our environment. Staying focused remains a complex issue. Discernment must be the ribbon that wraps around our life, keeping it protected and wholesome. Is this not an ideal life for us, our children, and our planet?

When miracles come there are no trumpets sounding or great winds blowing. They simply appear in silence. If you are not aware of them, then you may miss them. If you do not have a heart for God, then you may have always missed them. Miracles given to us open up our hearts to see God.

God's presence requires you to change your attitude and look at life from a different point of view, by seeing it through the softness of your eyes and heart. God is always seeking our attention because He needs us. So open up your arms to your Creator and remember that God gave you life. His love is mercy, grace, and compassion. His Comforter is here for you.

"Be still and know that I am here.
I always am.
Watch Me work."

"Child, dear child,
yes, now you know it all;
now you know what is to be.
You will remain here at least for a while.
How long depends on your growth.
You both have much to do now;

you all have My blessings.
Dig into your present and happy life.
You are now able to make the best of it.
Have not I given it to you before?
Was it not right in front of your eyes before?
But you turned from it; you turned from Me,
and went your lonely way refusing to hear
My voice to turn you around toward Me.
All that which you lived was not lost.
You have gained plenty from living the life you chose.
Now you have Me in direct line with yourself.
At times when you would have gone astray as before,
you did not.
You chose to stick to our narrow path,
which is the right and proper one.
Now you are on your way;
your head is straight; your thoughts are clear;
and your eyes are not wayward but steadfast
to the one thing in front of you,
Me.
Go, child, in peace now.
It is the one thing long overdue in you.
Sleep and be at rest.

You are well now, and all problems
have sorted themselves out and melted away.
It is your turn to shine, and shine you shall.
With My blessings,
you will rise higher and higher always.
I love you, child, as I love all."

Epilogue

GOD WILL NEVER LEAVE YOU

GOD ALWAYS SAID, "Look to the light, and you will see wonders.."

How could I see wonders with chaos all around me and my entire life falling apart? I never saw a wonder in my life! I was not even sure what a "wonder" was. How was I to get to that point? It was to become a journey of listening and seeking out the "wonders," and it took me a long time.

Each message took me years to understand, but it led me in the right direction. God was asking me to be positive and to look to the light. That is what led me out of the darkness. Even though my situation changed, and sometimes I felt worse than before, God never gave up on me. Speaking to my heart, God's Comforter gently guided me, moment by moment, day by day, and year by year.

God never, ever, gave up on me. He gave me the strength when I never had hope. He gave me a heart to see. Thank You, God, for what You have done for me. So please do it for others!

"I would, child, if they would only listen.
I am here, always.
You are My dream come true."

www.ingramcontent.com/pod-product-compliance
Ingram Content Group UK Ltd.
Pitfield, Milton Keynes, MK11 3LW, UK
UKHW020239250726
13967UKWH00001B/463